I0435241

Butterflies in Boise

An excursion through the fascinating life of butterflies

Written & photographed by
Erin A. Olsen

Butterflies in Boise
An excursion through the fascinating life of butterflies

Erin A. Olsen

FASCINATING FEATURES YOU'LL FIND INSIDE

From the Author...

I only recently started enjoying time visiting butterfly exhibits. I found there is nothing as enlightening as watching the simplicity of a butterfly, who knows nothing of the joy and delight it brings to the world, who cares not about the concerns or motivations of others, whose focus and purpose are pure as it flits from flower to flower completely oblivious to its own importance. There is nothing as refreshing as hearing young children exclaim that a butterfly is the most beautiful thing they've seen or how amazing they are, their exclamations having nothing to do with technology, texting or video games. There is nothing as joyous as the uninhibited giggle and ear-to-ear grin of a grown adult when they realize a butterfly has lit on their head. There is nothing as humbling as visiting communities who have acknowledged their needs and chosen to embrace the unique opportunities butterflies provide even though it requires changes to their traditional way of living in order to preserve nature for the betterment of all. There has been nothing more refreshing for my soul than butterflies and I am eager to share them with you.

BUTTERFLIES IN BOISE

Butterflies are one of nature's most beautiful and delicate creatures. To many people, they represent life, health, peace and harmony. They were depicted 3,500 years ago in Egyptian art and generate strong emotions regardless of how they are encountered.

The exact number is unknown. Generally it is agreed there are more than 18,000 species of butterflies in the world but occasionally a new species will be identified. Butterflies are found all over the world from the tropics to the arctic, on all continents except Antarctica. More butterfly species live at the equator where the temperature stays warm. Fewer species are found the farther from the equator you go.

Boise, Idaho is about 3,000 miles from the equator and 3,200 miles from the North Pole, making it halfway between the equator and North Pole. Boise enjoys warm summers and mild but cold winters, including snow. This means Boise doesn't have as many butterfly species as more tropical places but it still has a lot! There have

been 307 verified butterfly and moth species sighted in Idaho, including 170 different butterflies. 87 species have been verified in Ada county, which includes Boise.

The Monarch Butterfly is the official insect of the State of Idaho. It was made official in 1992. Monarchs must have milkweed plants to  survive. They lay their eggs on them. The caterpillars eat milkweed leaves. The sap from milkweed makes the caterpillars and butterflies poisonous so keeps them from being eaten by predators like birds. Milkweed can grow in deserts, grasslands and forests so there are many places in Idaho where Monarchs can live...but not in winter. Milkweed plants are dormant in winter so there are no leaves for the Monarchs. There are many other species of butterflies in Idaho. They all need some type of plant to live, just like the Monarchs. Because these plants can't live in Idaho in the winter, there are fewer butterfly species and those who do live here move to warmer places once it gets cold. In the spring and summer, if you are patient and look carefully, you can find butterflies in your yard, in parks, by rivers, in meadows and in the mountains around Idaho.

If you haven't had a chance to see butterflies or if you want to see tropical butterflies, there is an option. Each year, from June through August, butterflies can be seen in Boise that do not normally live here. They come from Costa Rica and are brought here as part of Zoo Boise's "Butterflies in Bloom" program. The walk-through display lets you get close, watch, experience and appreciate magnificent tropical butterflies.

BEAUTIFUL BUGS!

Did you know butterflies are bugs? Their colorful wings let people enjoy them as beautiful, graceful creatures and sometimes forget they are insects. Scientists classify things into groups. In the Animalia (animal) group there is a group called Arthropoda. In that group is the Insecta (insect) group. Butterflies are in the Insecta group and are related to bees, beetles and grasshoppers. They have the same body parts and life stages as other insects.

Animalia (kingdom)

Arthopoda (phylum)

Insecta (class)

BUTTERFLY BODIES

Humans and many other animals have a skeleton inside their body, especially their spine or backbone, and long bones in their arms and legs. Butterflies are **invertebrates** (in-**vur**-tuh-brits) which means they don't have a spine or bones. Instead, insects have a hard shell called an **exoskeleton** (ek-soh-**skel**-i-tn) on the outside of their body. It supports them, like our bones do. It protects them and keeps water inside so they don't dry out.

People and other mammals like dogs and cats, are **warm-blooded** (**wawrm bluhd**-id). This means their bodies always stay at the same temperature, no matter how warm or cold it gets. Many animals like snakes, frogs, fish and butterflies are **cold-blooded** (**kohld bluhd**-id). This means they can't control their body temperature.

Cold-blooded animals **bask** (bahsk) or lay in the sun to get warm. They might also lay on things like rocks that have been warmed by the sun, even after the sun goes down at night. Butterflies will find a sunny spot first thing in the morning and sit with their wings open wide to get warm.

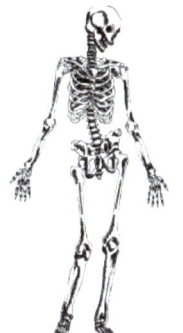 

Many animals, like people, have skeletons inside their body. Insects, like beetles & butterflies, have exoskeletons on the outside of their body.

THE HEAD

All insects, including butterflies, have bodies made up of three parts: head, abdomen and thorax. A butterfly's head, like other insects, has antennae and eyes.

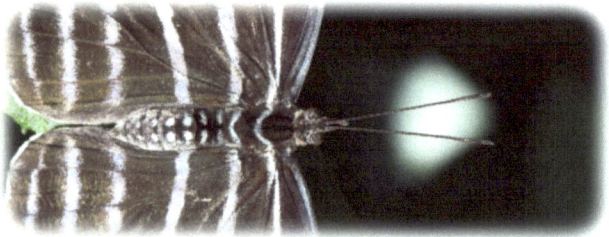

The Antennae

Butterflies have two **antennae** (an-**ten**-uh). Some people call them "feelers" but they are not used to feel things. Butterflies use them to "smell" the air. A butterfly's antennae are like a person's nose. Being able to smell is important to butterflies.

Butterflies can move their antennae to help them smell better. It's like when you lift your chin to smell something better. Butterflies can also move their antennae to help balance when they fly like using your arms to help balance when you walk across a rope or log.

Beyond the Basics

Antennae contain chemical receptors that allow butterflies to identify food or danger by the way they smell. Using them, a butterfly can determine, "that's a milkweed plant" or "that's a human!"

Butterflies can move or angle their antennae to suit their needs. They can angle them to smell better. You may see butterflies **"antennae dipping"** into dirt, leaves or fruit to sample it and help them determine what it is.

Antennae also help the butterfly balance during flight. It helps them compensate for wind or physical factors. This is especially helpful if their wings have been damaged. Adjusting their antennae is like a pilot adjusting the flaps on an airplane.

Both butterflies and airplanes need to stay in balance when they fly. Airplanes use many controls, including flaps. Butterflies use their antennae.

Compound Eyes

People have two eyes. They work together to see one picture at a time. Insects, including butterflies, also have two eyes, but they are **compound eyes** (**kom**-pound ahyz). That means it seems like they have two eyes, but each has many smaller eyes. To a butterfly, it's like looking at a wall of TV screens at the store all at the same time but with each one on a different channel.

Butterflies see a lot of things at one time, but they don't always see them very clearly. Scientists think they can see things close to them but not very far away. They can see light and dark, color and sense movement. They can see above, below, to the left and to the right. They can see in front of them and even behind them, but they can't see any one thing in detail. Their brains are small and don't let them understand things that way. They don't need to. They can see something big is coming. It doesn't matter exactly what it is, they just need to get away from it.

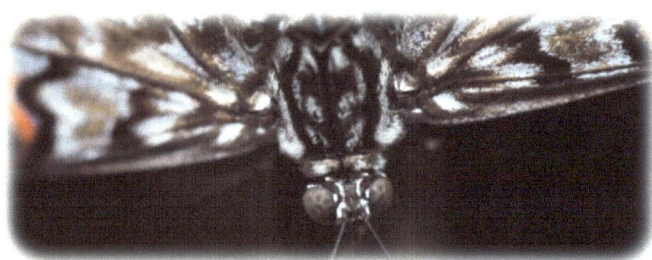

BUTTERFLY BIT

Butterflies can see red, yellow and green

Beyond the Basics

Butterflies have average vision. Their eyes are sensitive to light, color, patterns and movement but they don't get a clear picture of anything in particular. Scientists think butterflies can focus as close as ½". What is impressive is that they can process about 150 images per second. The average video plays at 30 frames per second, so butterflies are seeing five times as many images each second as people do watching a video. A butterfly's brain does very little processing or understanding of the visual information it receives though, compared to a human.

Compound eyes give butterflies an almost 360° field of view— up, down, left, right, forward and backward. They don't see one, single image. Instead, they see lots of individual ones, but with 150 of them each second from all directions, it's not easy to sneak up behind a butterfly!

They might not be able to think, "here comes a human hand with five fingers" but they do know something big is moving closer to them and can react appropriately.

Many insects can see two basic colors. Butterflies and humans can see three. By combining these three colors, we can perceive many colors. Humans can see colors of the rainbow, red to violet (ROYGBIV). These colors correspond to wavelengths. Unlike humans, butterflies can see higher frequency ultraviolet (UV) light too.

This is important because there are markings in nature that humans can't see. Many flowers have ultraviolet patterns on their petals that act for butterflies like runway lights do for airplanes. They let them find and line up correctly. These **nectar markers** (**nek**-ter **mahr**-kerz) guide butterflies to the nectar in a flower.

Female butterflies have UV overlays on their bodies. Male butterflies can see these markings. They allow them to mate more easily.

Many scientists believe the colors on butterflies that we see as so beautiful are for other animals. They act as either a warning or as camouflage. Butterflies themselves don't use these visual colors nearly as much as they rely on ultraviolet markings on plants and other butterflies.

Runway lights let pilots line up correctly so they can land safely. Image courtesy of NASA (http://images.ksc.nasa.gov).

Mimulus flower photographed in visible light (left) and ultraviolet light (right) showing nectar guides, visible to butterflies but not humans. Used by permission from Plantsurger via the WikiMedia Commons (http://commons.wikimedia.org/wiki/ File:Mimulus_nectar_guide_UV_VIS.jpg)

The "Cleo" butterfly (Gonepteryx Cleopatra) as seen in normal, visible light (left) and using special ultraviolet light techniques (right). Images courtesy of Dr. Klaus Schmitt (Weinheim, Germany). For more information, please visit http://photographyoftheinvisibleworld.blogspot.com/2012/07/ gonepteryx-cleopatra-cleo-butterfly-on.html.

The Proboscis

Unlike other insects, butterflies don't have jaws or **mandibles** (**man**-duh-buh-lz). Butterflies can't chew. Instead of lips, a mouth and teeth, they have a **proboscis** (proh-**bos**-is) which is like a straw they sip through. They keep their proboscis rolled up underneath their head until they want to drink, then they unroll it to take a sip. When done, they roll it up out of the way.

The proboscis can be up to one and a half times the butterfly's length. It needs to be long enough to reach the nectar in whatever flower the butterfly drinks from.

If their proboscis gets clogged, it can be "unlinked" into two sections so each can be cleared. If you've ever drank a milkshake or smoothie and gotten a clump of something stuck in your straw, you know what this is like. If a butterfly's proboscis gets clogged and can't be opened, the butterfly will starve.

Butterflies keep their proboscis rolled up (top). They unroll it to sip from flowers or fruit (right) or to sip water from wet sand (top right)

THE THORAX

The middle section of a butterfly's body is its **thorax** (**thohr**-aks). The wings and legs are attached to the thorax.

The Legs

All insects have six legs. All butterflies have six legs. Butterflies only use four legs for walking, so it might look like they have four. The front legs are only used to clean the antennae.

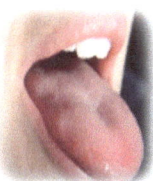

Butterflies taste with their feet. They scratch a petal or leaf to taste it and decide if it's a good place to lay eggs or find a drink. A butterfly's feet are like a human's tongue.

Beyond the Basics

A butterfly's legs are divided into three pairs: fore, middle and hind. Each leg has five joints. The last joint has a "claw" for holding on. The middle and hind legs are used for walking. The forelegs can't be used for walking. They are usually held up and out of the way, often making them hard to identify.

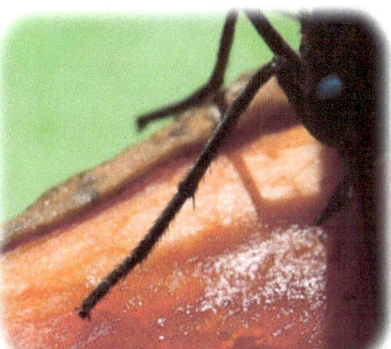

Butterflies have six legs, each with five segments. The last segment can look like a foot, but it's not.

The Wings

All butterflies have four wings – two in the front and two in the back. Their wings come in many shapes and sizes. Some butterflies can be as wide as a grape while others are as wide as a watermelon. Sometimes butterflies are grouped by the color or shape of their wings.

Scientists sometimes use special names to identify things. One of the scientific names for butterflies is **Lepidoptera** (lep-i-**dop**-ter-uh). It means "wings with scales". Butterflies have tiny scales on their wings like fish have scales. The scales have different shapes and colors.

The basic colors of butterfly scales include black, red and yellow. Different species of butterflies look like they have different colors because they mix different colors of scales. It's like mixing two colors of paint. If you mix red and yellow, you get orange. A butterfly with red and yellow scales might look orange.

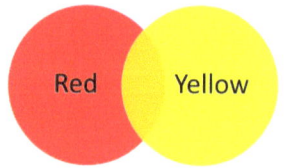

Because butterfly wings are covered with scales, they are fragile. Scales can be rubbed off very easily. This damages their wings. They are often damaged by predators and people but can be damaged by everyday use too. There's good news though! Even if a large part of a butterfly's wings are damaged, they can often still fly.

BUTTERFLY BIT

Butterflies vary in width from a tiny 1/4" to a huge 12"

Beyond the Basics

Butterflies have different types of scales. **Pigmentary scales** (**pig**-muh-n-ter-ee skeylz) grow like hair and

fingernails grow in people. These scales contain melanin which is brown and black. Scales can also contain other materials of certain colors: uric acid (white), carotenoids (yellow, orange) and flavonoids (red, purple). These scales create basic butterfly colors.

A butterfly's wing membrane is transparent. Pigmentary scales add the color. Each scale can be a different color. If a butterfly's wing seems transparent, it doesn't have many pigmentary scales. What appears to be the variety of colors come from the amount of pigment in individual scales, how scales are layered with other colors and how densely the scales are arranged. Scales also have different shapes – rectangles, teardrops and even plumes.

Structural scales (**struhk**-cher-uhl skeylz) don't have any color and are semi-transparent or partially see-through. They diffract and refract light like a prism. They are responsible for the amazing metallic and iridescent colors of some butterflies. Colors produced structurally (instead of by pigments) are more intense and bright.

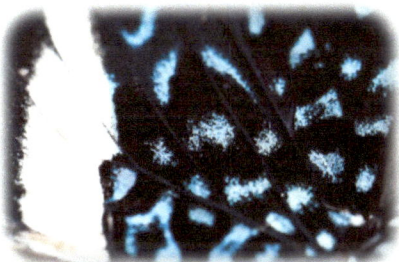
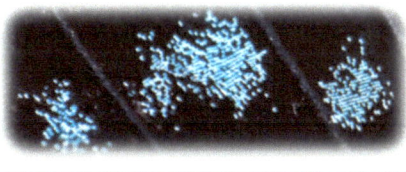

Colored butterfly wings aren't smooth, they're covered with scales.

The colors of butterfly wings have many purposes. They protect them from predators. Bright colors signal, "I'm poisonous" or "I taste bad." Some colors provide camouflage. Some patterns confuse predators. Others help find mates. They are more than just pretty colors.

Vessels (veins) in wings make them rigid or stiff. Veins come from the thorax at the base of the wings. The pattern of the veins is different for each species.

BUTTERFLY BIT

Butterfly wings can have 600 scales per millimeter

Color makes butterflies beautiful but also has a purpose. It can signal not to eat them (top). It can provide camouflage (left). Sometimes camouflage isn't to hide but to confuse, like the "eye spot" on some species (middle right). If a butterfly's wings don't have many scales, they look transparent (bottom).

Backlight helps you see the four wings and veins more easily (top). Colors can be intense (middle right). Some pilots report seeing blue morphos (middle left) from 1/2 mile away when they fly over rainforests. Butterfly wings are delicate but even damaged (bottom) they can usually still fly.

THE ABDOMEN

Butterflies are animals, like humans. Their bodies must do some of the same things the human body does. Butterflies need to breathe, digest food, move fluids and make babies so they have respiratory, digestive, circulatory and reproductive systems. Unlike people, they are very simple in butterflies and are all found in the 3rd segment of their body, the **abdomen** (**ab**-doh-mu-n).

Since liquids (nectar, juice and water) are the only things butterflies eat, liquids are the only thing that must be digested and gotten rid of as waste. Using words we know, that means butterflies pee but they don't poop.

There is a lot to learn about exactly how butterflies breathe, digest, manage their bodily fluids, temperature and reproduce. The study of butterflies is called **lepidopterology** (lep-i-dop-tuh-**rol**-uh-jee) and scientists who study them are **lepidopterists**.(lep-i-dop-tuh-**rists**).

BUTTERFLIES VS. MOTHS

Butterflies and moths are very similar. They are both insects. They are both *Lepidoptera*. It might be hard to tell the difference at first but there are unique differences.

- ❀ Most butterflies fold their wings above their back while resting. Most moths leave their wings open.

- ❀ Most butterflies have brightly colored wings. Most moths are plain brown, gray, white or black.

- ❀ Most butterflies have fine scales on their wings. Moths have larger scales so look "fuzzier" than butterflies.

- ❀ Most butterflies have thinner bodies than moths.

- ❀ Most butterflies are active during the daytime. Most moths are active at night. Animals that are active during the day are called **diurnal** (dahy-**ur**-nl) and those active at night are **nocturnal** (nok-**tur**-nl).

- ❀ Most butterfly antennae have little knobs on the ends. Moth antennae are either plain or feathery. Because of this, one of the names for butterflies means "clubbed horn" and for moths means "varied horn".

- ❀ Both butterflies and moths undergo complete metamorphosis but butterflies build a **chrysalis** (**kris**-uh-lis) and moths build a cocoon (kuh-**koon**).

- ❀ Chrysalises hang. Cocoons rest or lay on something.

- ❀ There are about 12 times more species of moths than butterflies: about 250,000 moths vs. 18,000 butterflies.

These are the common differences but with thousands of species, there are exceptions to these general guidelines.

THE BUTTERFLY LIFE CYCLE

People start life as a baby, then become toddlers, school-aged children and adolescents before finally becoming adults. Butterflies go through different life phases too. There are four stages.

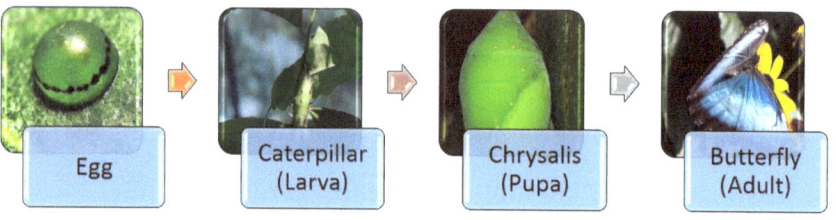

| Egg | Caterpillar (Larva) | Chrysalis (Pupa) | Butterfly (Adult) |

The four stages of the butterfly life cycle. These are Blue Morpho butterflies.

The Egg

Butterflies start as eggs. Female butterflies lay eggs on a specific type of plant that they know their caterpillars will eat. This is called a **host plant**. Different butterflies require different host plants. Many species can only use one type of host plant. Without a host plant, caterpillars will starve.

Butterfly eggs laid as clusters on leaves of host plants

Beyond the Basics

Butterflies are identified by wing shape and coloration. Different species have specific and distinct markings. When males and females within a species have different colors and patterns, it's called **dimorphism** (dahy-**mawr**-fiz-uh-m). Some butterfly species are dimorphic. The differentiation between male and female happens very early in the development of an egg.

Shortly after an egg is laid, it begins to develop. Cells split into two cells. This is called **mitosis** (mahy-**toh**-sis). Occasionally, when the egg has just been laid and only has the very first few cells, those cells don't divide correctly. The result is that one of the new cells has male traits and the other has female traits. This is called **gynandromorphism** (ji-**nan**-druh-mawrf-ism). It's a long word for something that happens fairly often in butterflies and insects. Sometimes it even happens in birds.

There are two forms of gynandromorph butterflies. If the butterfly has female markings on one side and male markings on the other, it's called **bilateral asymmetry** (**bahy**-lat-er-uhl ey-**sim**-i-tree). If the two blend into a new pattern that's the same on both sides, it's called a **mosaic** (moh-**zey**-ik). You might think it's a new species but it's not. It's interesting to see and it happened when the egg was first developing.

A bilaterally asymmetrical gynandromorph Blue-frosted Banner (Catonephele numilia) butterfly

The Larva — Caterpillar

The 2nd phase of a butterfly's life is the **larval** (**lahr**-vl) stage. Butterfly larva are called **caterpillars** (**kat**-er-pil-erz). The first thing a caterpillar does when it hatches is crawl out of the egg shell and eat the egg shell.

After the egg shell, caterpillars start to eat the host plant. Their only job is to eat. Because of this, they have to be able to move to find leaves to eat. Caterpillars have six legs. It looks like they have more but these are not real legs. They are called **prolegs**. Caterpillars can have up to five pairs of prolegs on their abdomen. The three pair of legs on the thorax are true legs. They will keep the true legs when they change to butterflies, but not the prolegs. Caterpillar legs have hooks so they can "stick" to leaves like Velcro®.

If you watch a caterpillar, it looks like it moves in a wave. They move starting with the back set of legs. Then, each pair of legs reaches forward, one set at a time, from the back to the front. A lot goes on inside when it moves too. A caterpillar can have as many as 4,000 muscles in its

small body. Humans only have 629 muscles in a much larger body. Caterpillars have about 248 muscles just in their head with another 70 or so in each body segment. Many of these muscles help the caterpillar move and eat.

Caterpillars eat a lot. They are similar to human teenagers who eat and grow a lot too. Some caterpillars eat 27,000 times their body weight in just a few weeks!

While a caterpillar's insides grow, its outside does not. When a caterpillar becomes too big for its skin, it **molts** (mohltz). The skin splits and falls off, exposing a new skin. As it eats and grows, a caterpillar molts five or six times.

Caterpillars have many strategies to survive. Some eat plants that have chemicals that make them taste bad so predators don't want to eat them. Caterpillars also have a gland on the bottom of their head. It squirts a liquid that turns to silk when exposed to air. The silk can be used as a "safety line" in case the caterpillar falls off a leaf. They can also use it to hang off a leaf, in case of danger, like someone in a movie swinging from the roof of a building.

BUTTERFLY BIT

If a human grew at the same rate as a caterpillar, at one month old it would be bigger than a double-decker bus

The Pupa — Chrysalis

After a caterpillar grows, it enters the 3rd or **pupal** (**pyoo**-puhl) stage. First, it empties its stomach. The pupa is only about half as big as the caterpillar because half of a caterpillar body is stomach! The caterpillar then uses its silk strands to spin a sack called a **chrysalis** (**kris**-uh-lis). It's like rolling yourself up inside a blanket so you're snug and protected. The chrysalis hardens. Metamorphosis begins.

Metamorphosis (met-uh-**mawr**-fuh-sis) means "to change shape". Inside the chrysalis, parts of the caterpillar's body that aren't needed anymore are formed into new parts the butterfly will use. Simple eyes become compound eyes. The caterpillar's mouth becomes the butterfly's proboscis. Antennae and wings form. It's like when a magician steps into a box and a woman steps out. A caterpillar wraps up in the chrysalis and a butterfly emerges. Metamorphosis is very scientific but like the magic trick, metamorphosis *seems* magical.

Metamorphosis can take a week to several months. The average is two weeks to a month. The day before a butterfly is ready to emerge, the chrysalis gets translucent or partly see-through. At this time, the pattern of the butterfly's wings can be seen from the outside.

Butterfly keepers "pin" chrysalis so they can monitor their development

The Adult — Butterfly

When the time is right, the 4th phase begins as a new adult butterfly wiggles and pushes from inside the chrysalis.

When it emerges, it crawls to a sunny spot. It needs to warm up and let its wings spread and dry. This takes an hour or two. The butterfly also needs to assemble its proboscis. It starts out in two pieces. It will curl and uncurl the proboscis to test it. The butterfly will also exercise its wings by moving them slowly up and down.

Once it feels strong, the butterfly will fly to find food and a mate. Caterpillars grow...a lot. Butterflies don't grow. When they emerge, they are the size they'll be the rest of their life.

Butterfly keepers often move newly hatched adult butterflies to an emergence box. This protects them until they are ready to fly. They are placed at the bottom of the box. After their wings harden and they warm up, they crawl to the top where they can exercise their wings before taking flight for the first time.

Beyond the Basics

Butterflies usually emerge in the morning to maximize time in the sun. When they emerge, their body is fat with fluid and the wings are wrinkled and wet. The butterfly pumps the fluid from its body to its wings. It hangs upside down so gravity can help move the fluid. If a wing gets caught during this process and can't fully stretch, it will harden malformed. If that happens, the butterfly may never be able to fly. During this time, the butterfly is helpless. Everything must happen correctly. This is critical for the butterfly to be able to survive — to eat, fly and reproduce.

A recently emerged butterfly has pushed the fluid from its body to its wings. The wings have spread, dried and stiffened. After crawling to the top of an emergence box, it spends time slowly exercising its wings before taking flight.

Note: Images on these pages captured at Victoria Butterfly Gardens (British Columbia, Canada)

BUTTERFLY BIT: WHAT DO YOU CALL A GROUP OF BUTTERFLIES?

A lot of insects found in one place at one time is often called a swarm. Since butterflies are insects, a group of them can also be called a swarm but "swarm" sounds scary to a lot of people. There are other names you might want to use instead. They better describe the beauty and nature of butterflies who gather to migrate, mate and sometimes just to communicate socially. What word do you like?

A "flight"

A "flutter"

A "rabble"

A "kaleidoscope"

Butterfly Reproduction

In nature, finding food is always important. Other than that, the main job of an adult butterfly is to reproduce. Female butterflies spend most of their time looking for the right host plant on which they can lay their eggs. Male butterflies spend most of their time looking for females.

Females lay eggs on a host plant. Most butterflies can only use one type of plant as a host. If they can't find these plants, they can't lay their eggs.

Butterflies can start laying eggs within hours after emerging from the chrysalis. Some lay all their eggs at once. Others lay their eggs over several days.

Butterflies use different strategies to try to protect their eggs. Some lay them on the *bottom* of leaves so flying predators can't see them. Others lay them in large batches so if one is damaged, the others may be OK. This is the "strength in numbers" strategy. Others lay only one at a time in any given spot so if one is found or damaged, others in different places will be OK. This is the "don't put all your eggs on one leaf" strategy. Some butterflies use camouflage to hide eggs. They might lay one at a time on the *top* of leaves so they look like water drops and not eggs. Butterflies use many strategies to help protect their eggs so they can mature and hatch as caterpillars.

Beyond the Basics

Many female butterflies produce scents that attract males. They are called **pheromones** (**fer**-uh-mohnz). It's like when girls wear perfume. These scents often smell like the flowers the butterflies are attracted to. Males can smell these scents up to a mile away. That's like being able to smell a flower at the Boise train depot from the steps of the capitol building!

Many male butterflies compete for the attention of a female. Mating can take several hours. The female will then search for the right host plant and squeeze the eggs from her egg sack. As the eggs pass, they are fertilized by the sperm held in a special pouch after mating. When an egg is laid, it has been fertilized for only a few seconds. The eggs are attached to the leaves of the host plant where they develop until the caterpillar larva emerges.

Female butterflies will lay eggs even if they haven't been fertilized. Unfortunately, many eggs will never hatch. The eggs are very delicate and can be damaged before the caterpillars have a chance to develop. Eggs can get too dry. If they stay too wet, they can get moldy. Birds, ants and wasps will eat butterfly eggs too.

BUTTERFLY BIT

On average, butterflies lay a total of 150 - 200 eggs in their lifetime

THE BUTTERFLY LIFESPAN

How long butterflies live depends on many things: temperature, food, predators, disease and more. The average lifespan of a butterfly is one month. With thousands of species, it varies from as short as a few days to as long as nine months.

Large vs. Small

- In general, larger butterflies live longer
- Smaller butterflies are easier prey
- More things are dangerous for a small butterfly

Warm vs. Cold

- Butterflies can't live if it's too cold
- If they emerge late in the summer they may not live as long because it gets too cold
- Some eggs and pupa will hibernate or wait until it's warm enough to hatch or emerge

Captive vs. Wild

- Wild butterflies are often eaten by predators
- Wild butterflies may not find enough food
- Wild butterflies may get cold or catch diseases
- In an enclosure, butterflies are taken care of

The number of individuals that make it from egg to butterfly is very small. The number that do *not* live to reproduce as an adult is called the **mortality rate** (mawr-**tal**-i-tee reyt) and is about 98%. That means, on average, only two or three eggs laid by a male/female pair will complete the full life cycle and result in them laying fertilized eggs to ensure the next generation.

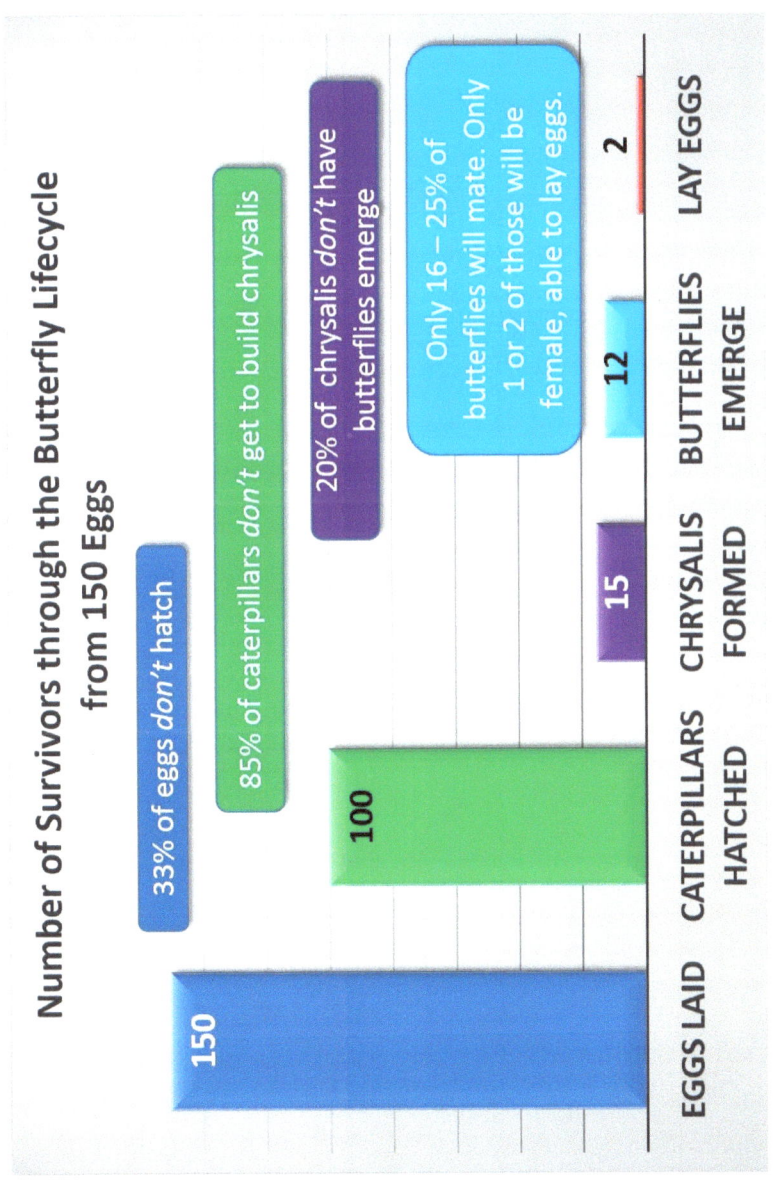

Number of Survivors through the Butterfly Lifecycle from 150 Eggs

33% of eggs *don't* hatch

85% of caterpillars *don't* get to build chrysalis

20% of chrysalis *don't* have butterflies emerge

Only 16 – 25% of butterflies will mate. Only 1 or 2 of those will be female, able to lay eggs.

150 · 100 · 15 · 12 · 2

EGGS LAID · CATERPILLARS HATCHED · CHRYSALIS FORMED · BUTTERFLIES EMERGE · LAY EGGS

BUTTERFLY FLIGHT

Butterflies have four wings, two in the front and two in the back. They are not connected but they move together. The butterfly uses muscles in its thorax to move its wings but since butterflies are cold-blooded, if they are too cold, their flight muscles can't work.

How *anything* can fly is complicated. Butterflies use many of the same techniques as airplanes. They create lift by touching their wings together then quickly separating them, rotating them at the same time to make a swirl of air. They use that swirl of air to move forward.

With each wing flap, butterflies move more air than they need to stay up. This makes it look like they "flit" instead of flying smoothly. This makes it harder for predators to see them. It's also why the Sioux Indian word for butterfly means "fluttering wings".

 BUTTERFLY BIT

The top butterfly flight speed
is 12 miles per hour (mph).
Some moths can fly 25 mph.
Butterflies can't fly if it's below 55°,
The best temperature is 82° - 100°.

BUTTERFLY MIGRATION

Many animals must move in order to find food or keep warm during the winter. This type of movement is called **migration** (mayh-**grey**-shuhn). Some butterflies migrate. Idaho gets cold in winter. Flowers can't grow in cold weather. Some butterflies who live in Idaho need to migrate to keep warm and have food.

Sometimes butterflies that live in warm areas migrate too. Why? Because if they live in one place too long, the caterpillars will eat all of the leaves they need for food. Without enough host plants, butterflies can't reproduce.

Some butterflies that live in areas that get cold don't migrate either. Their eggs or chrysalis **hibernate** (**hi**-ber-neyt) through the cold weather. They basically sleep through the winter and only hatch when it's warm. This way, they can live their entire life in one place.

Monarch butterflies are famous for their migrations to Mexico and California. Each year, they migrate south during the winter and north in the summer. Monarchs migrate thousands of miles, sometimes as far north as Canada. Their massive numbers during migration form clouds of color, often a mile wide and a mile long.

Many butterflies don't live long enough to migrate both ways. It can take two or three generations to complete the trip. None of them has made the trip before but butterflies somehow find a way to follow the same migration route to the same destination every year.

BUTTERFLY DRINKS

Caterpillars only eat leaves. The leaves provide all the nutrients they need to grow before transforming into a butterfly. During metamorphosis, the caterpillar's jaws become the butterfly's proboscis so butterflies can only sip liquids. They can't chew so they sip **nectar** (**nek**-ter) from flowers, juice from fruit and water.

In some environments, it's hard to find water. Some butterflies have to get creative to find it. Some get water and minerals from mud and wet sand. Some sip tree sap. It may not sound good to us, but some butterflies sip from animal dung and decaying **carcasses** (**kahr**-kuhs-iz).

Nectar comes from flowers and is another name for juices of fruits. There are so many flowers in the world it's impossible to name them all but in general, butterflies prefer clusters of small flowers with a shape that has a good landing platform. Butterflies are active during the day, so they look for brightly colored flowers especially red, yellow or orange. The blooms must be open during the day too. The best flowers make lots of nectar.

Butterflies like soft, juicy fruits too. They will drink from bananas, oranges, watermelon and many other fruits.

Quality butterfly exhibits provide both flowers and fruit for the butterflies. They also provide water sources. All are necessary for healthy butterflies.

BUTTERFLY BENEFITS

Butterflies aren't only beautiful, they are an important part of the food chain or web of life. Caterpillars eat leaves which helps recycle nutrients for other plants and animals. Some caterpillars eat plants that are considered weeds. This helps control weeds and keeps people who don't like weeds happy too.

Butterflies also help plants and flowers by moving pollen between plants and **pollinating** (**pol**-uh-neyt-ing) them. Without pollination, many plants can't reproduce.

Bees, hummingbirds, bats and moths are pollinators too. Butterflies are not as efficient as bees. When butterflies drink, they don't interact with the right parts of the flower. Because butterflies stand up on their legs, they don't brush up against pollen. Pollen doesn't stick well to their legs or proboscis either. There are some exceptions to this. Moths are better pollinators than most butterflies but some butterflies play an important part in pollination. Monarch butterflies, for example, transfer the pollen of milkweed plants very well.

The "food chain" means some plants and animals are eaten by other animals. They aren't "enemies" or "bad" but a necessary part of nature. Butterflies at all stages of their life cycle have **predators** (**pred**-uh-terz) who try to eat them. Some butterfly eggs get eaten, providing an important food source for animals like frogs and spiders. Caterpillars contain a lot of protein so are good food sources for other insects and animals like birds.

Caterpillars and butterflies are an important food source for other insects, snakes, mice and lizards. Without caterpillars and butterflies, many other animals would not have enough to eat. Predators should not be seen as bad but just part of what keeps nature in balance.

In some parts of the world, caterpillars and butterflies are eaten by humans. Before you say "ew, yuck", know that caterpillars are very high in protein and fat, more even than beef, fish or lentils. They are loaded with nutrients. For some people, they are an important food source.

Butterflies are so intertwined with their environment (plants, flowers and other organisms), that they are good indicators of the health of an entire ecosystem. Scientists often look to butterflies as indicators of air, water, soil, plant and animal health. If the environment is not in balance, plants, for example, will decrease and the butterflies that rely on them for host plants and nectar will also decrease so scientists can monitor the health of an ecosystem based on the populations of butterflies. In addition to being beautiful and tranquil, butterflies play an important role in nature as a whole.

BUTTERFLY CONSERVATION

Butterflies have existed for millions of years but in the last 200 years about 10% of the world's butterfly species have become **extinct** (ik-**stinght**). This means there are no more anywhere on earth. As with so many plants and animals, the main threat to butterflies is loss of habitat. If the area where they can find suitable host plants and flowers is smaller or gone, not as many butterflies can live.

People are usually the cause of habitat loss. Clearing land for farming, using chemicals to grow food, polluting air and water and physically building where forests, fields and grasslands once were all reduce or destroy habitat.

Many butterfly host plants are considered weeds so people remove them because they don't like them, even if they aren't building something. They replace them with what *people* consider prettier plants but without host plants, butterflies can't reproduce. If this happens, butterflies might move to other places. If there's no other place to go, eventually they become extinct.

BUTTERFLY BIT

There are more types of insects in one tropical rain forest tree than there are in the entire state of Vermont

Conservation: The care, protection, preservation or restoration from change including damage, neglect, decay, exploitation and loss

Work to conserve butterflies and their habitats has been started. Research is important to understand the thousands of species. People need to know how to protect them. Educating the public on how they can help preserve and restore butterfly habitat is also important. It takes good information and people willing to work for butterflies in order to ensure they survive into the future.

THE BUTTERFLY BUSINESS

In some places, people feel they need to destroy butterfly habitat in order to live. Butterflies offer a different way for people to make a living. Instead of cutting down forests for logging, agriculture and development, they can use the forest, protect habitat and make a decent living by raising butterflies.

Costa Rica is a country in Central America where they have embraced conservation. Although fairly small in size, Costa Rica is a world leader in conservation. A substantial and remarkable 33% of the country is protected as refuges, reserves and national parks.

Costa Rica has also developed their butterfly business in order to help their economy, provide education to the world about the importance and beauty of butterflies and preserve their own natural resources. This effort is not run by mega-corporations but by small businesses that help support their own struggling communities known as "socially inclusive enterprises".

Some places people live, they can enjoy butterflies in the wild. Other people who live in cities or colder places either can't see them or just not nearly as many as warmer, more rural locations. Many tourist destinations, especially in the tropics, have butterfly exhibits so tourists can see them more easily. The exhibits are often farms too. Farms raise butterflies to sell. That way, organizations that want to display butterflies but don't have access to them, can buy butterfly chrysalis from the butterfly farms.

Central America's first commercial butterfly farm was Costa Rica Entomological Supply (CRES) in 1984. They opened to the public in 1990. CRES still sells butterflies for exhibits but also provides visitor viewing and education.

CRES and other butterfly farms are a source of income to poor and developing communities. They allow people with limited resources to start a business and learn skills. They provide a unique product that can't be easily reproduced. They allow people to see and learn, and organizations to exhibit and educate, who otherwise couldn't. They let people enjoy a few moments of simple natural beauty. They protect species and ecosystems. Like butterflies, these farms play an important role in nature and society.

In Costa Rica, the Doka Estate coffee plantation houses a butterfly exhibit for visitors (top). Oscar Cruz Hernandez is a butterfly keeper at the Mariposario Butterfly Farm at the Punta Leona Resort (right & bottom).

Zoo Boise

BUTTERFLIES IN BLOOM

Zoos have existed for centuries. For a long time, they displayed animals for the enjoyment of visitors, usually in cities and usually in very unnatural ways. The philosophy and role of responsible zoos has changed dramatically. Their priority now focuses on education and conservation. Some even act as rescue and rehabilitation facilities. Their purpose is no longer to just display animals for human enjoyment, but to preserve them in our world.

Zoo Boise has not only kept pace with this progressive philosophy, they are one of the nation's top zoo supporters of conservation. An important part of conservation is education. Zoo Boise's mission includes education and conservation as well as recreation. They work to be a place where people can learn about nature and conservation issues and become involved in making a difference. One of those projects is the annual "Butterflies in Bloom" exhibit that brings Costa Rican butterflies to Boise every June through August.

The exhibit and its maintenance may appear simple but the logistics of successfully carrying it out are complex. It begins with landscaping the enclosure. Once the enclosure is prepared, it's ready for butterflies!

The butterflies are purchased from CRES in Costa Rica and shipped to the Boise site. They are placed into an environmentally controlled room until they emerge. When this happens, the butterfly is allowed to go through its own natural process of emerging, stretching its wings and letting them harden. After an hour or two, when they are ready, they are released into the enclosure.

It's important to realize that although butterflies exist around the world, these butterflies are *not* native to Idaho. Therefore, they must be carefully and closely tracked. When visitors leave the exhibit, a "hitchhiker check" happens to be sure none have landed on a visitor and are about to be taken outside the enclosure. Naturally, the zoo doesn't want to lose any of its butterflies but it's also because a non-native species can cause problems with the balance of the local ecosystem. Non-native species simply should not be introduced into an environment in which they don't naturally live. This includes the beautiful but "visiting" Costa Rican butterflies. From the number of chrysalis received, to the number that hatch (and even those that do not) to the number of butterflies that live their life and expire in the enclosure, they must all be carefully accounted for and reported to the U.S. Department of Agriculture (USDA).

The Butterflies in Bloom enclosure is prepared with plants and flowers so the butterflies have nectar to sip and shade to protect them from the elements. There are purposefully no host plants for any of the species. This ensures the butterflies cannot reproduce. Visitors will never be able to see butterfly eggs or caterpillars in the enclosure. This is not the purpose of this exhibit and it's not allowed by the USDA.

Plates of fruit are placed throughout the enclosure. This is an important food source for the butterflies. It also provides a great opportunity for visitors to see them using their proboscis. You'll never see a butterfly eating fruit! Butterflies don't *eat* fruit, they can only *sip* the juice.

Costa Rica is humid. Boise is not. The butterflies have water sources in the enclosure including a fountain that is run when the enclosure is not open to the public. It also has a lot of dirt. We think of dirt as being dry but the soil in the planting beds are wetted each day. They're never made muddy, but moistened enough to give the butterflies moisture they can sip and to get cool if needed.

Butterflies live well in enclosures. Even in the protected area, there are some dangers. The main one is the visitors themselves. Excited people sometimes pick up the butterflies and damage their wings. Some people get scared and swat at them. Sometimes, butterflies bask or land on the path and get stepped on if people don't watch their feet as they walk. The butterfly keeper and volunteers do their best to protect the butterflies, but accidents do happen.

Some natural predators are present too. Wasps and hornets sometimes enter the enclosure to get to the butterflies. If these natural predators are found, they are usually removed from the enclosure.

The natural lifespan of many of the butterflies in the exhibit is only a few weeks. The exhibit is open for three months. Zoo Boise does not allow the butterflies to reproduce naturally by making sure no host plants are available. That means the butterflies must be replenished throughout the summer. Shipments of chrysalis are sent from Costa Rica every week throughout the summer to keep the butterfly numbers and variety required for the public to enjoy.

Butterflies in Bloom is only available three months each year. During that time, thousands of people flock to Zoo Boise to see them. For some, it is their first encounter with butterflies. For many, it's the closest they've ever been able to see them. For most, it's the first time they've seen Costa Rican butterflies. For everyone, it's a memorable experience most people never get to enjoy. Fortunately, the people of Boise and visitors to the city have the chance for a few months each summer!

WHAT DOES THAT MEAN?

- **Abdomen** (ab-doh-mu-n, noun) - the 3rd and last segment of a butterfly's body, behind the thorax, that contains the respiratory, digestive, circulatory and reproductive systems

- **Antennae** (an-ten-uh, noun) - a movable part on the heads of inserts and most arthropods that allows them to sense the air around them

- **Antennae dipping** (an-ten-uh dip-ing, verb) - moving antennae to touch an object to figure out what it is

- **Bask** (bahsk, verb) - to lie or purposefully position and expose oneself to warmth or heat

- **Bilateral asymmetry** (bahy-lat-er-uhl ey-sim-i-tree, noun) - when the left and right sides are not the same

- **Carcass** (kahr-kuhs, noun) - the dead body of an animal

- **Caterpillar** (kat-er-pil-er, noun) - the worm-like larva of a butterfly or moth and the 2nd stage of the butterfly life cycle

- **Chrysalis** (kris-uh-lis, noun) - the hard-shelled pupa of a butterfly during the 3rd stage of its life

- **Cocoon** (kuh-koon, noun) - the silky covering of the pupa during the lifecycle of many insects and moths

✿ **Cold-blooded** (kohld-bluhd-id, adjective) - animals whose body temperature changes based on the temperature of their environment

✿ **Compound eye** (kom-pound ahy, noun) - eyes that contain many smaller eyes or visual receptors called ommatidia, and common in arthropods, insects and crustaceans

✿**Dimorphism** (dahy-mawr-fiz-uh-m, noun) - two forms of the same species, being different in color or structure

✿**Diurnal** (dahy-ur-nl, adjective) - active during the daytime

✿**Dormant** (dawr-muh-nt, adjective) - inactive or if as asleep with no growth

✿**Exoskeleton** (ek-soh-skel-i-tn, noun) - an outside covering, usually hard, that provides protection and support

✿**Extinct** (ik-stingkt, adjective) - no longer exists as in there are no more of a species known to be on earth

✿**False leg** (fawls leg, noun) - Unjointed, extensions from the abdomen of caterpillars that look like true legs (which are jointed and found on the thorax), but are not. Also known as prolegs.

✿**Gynandromorph** (ji-nan-druh-mawrf, noun) - an individual displaying both male and female characteristics

Hibernate (hi-ber-neyt, verb) - to spend a period of time, usually in winter, in an inactive, sleep-like state, requiring little bodily functions and no growth

Host plant (hohst plahnt, noun) - the specific plant required by butterflies onto which they lay their eggs (1st life stage) and what the caterpillar (2nd life stage) eats after it emerges from the egg

Invertebrate (in-vur-tuh-brit, adjective) - without a backbone

Larva (lahr-vuh, noun) - the immature, wingless, feeding stage of an insect known as a caterpillar during the 2nd stage of the butterfly life cycle

Lepidoptera (lep-i-dop-ter-uh, noun) - The scientific order of insects that includes butterflies and moths

Lepidopterist (lep-i-dop-tuh-rist, noun) - a person who studies butterflies and moths

Lepidopterology (lep-i-dop-tuh-rol-uh-jee, noun) - the part of branch of zoology that deals with butterflies and moths

Mandible (man-duh-buh-l, noun) - in arthropods and insects, the mouthpart used for chewing, piercing or sucking

Metamorphosis (met-uh-mawr-fuh-sis, noun) - a profound change in an organism, usually from one life stage to another such as when a caterpillar goes through the pupal stage and emerges as an adult butterfly

Migration (mahy-grey-shuhn, noun) - movement of individuals, often as a group, from one area to another, at regular intervals or times of year

Mitosis (mahy-toh-sis, noun) - a method of cell division where the original cell splits into two identical new cells

Molt (mohlt, verb) - to shed the outer covering which will be replaced by new growth

Mortality rate (mawr-tal-i-tee rayt, noun) - the number of individuals that do not live through their full life cycle, in the case of butterflies, the number that die before being able to reproduce

Mosaic (moh-zey-ik, noun) - a type of gynandromorph butterfly where the male and female patterns are blended together with the same pattern on both wings

Nectar (nek-ter, noun) - the sugary liquid made by flowers that many insects and especially butterflies, like to drink

Nectar marker (nek-ter mahr-ker, noun) - an ultraviolet pattern on plants that guides or points to the part of the plant where the sugary secretions many animals eat can be found

Nocturnal (nok-tur-nl, adjective) - active at night

Pheromone (fer-uh-mohn, noun) - a chemical substance released by animals to attract members of the same species but of the opposite sex

Pigmentary scale (pig-muh-n-ter-ee skeyl, noun) - a thin, flat colored plate that covers butterfly wings

Pollinate (pol-uh-neyt, verb) - to move or carry pollen to a flower

Predator (pred-uh-ter, noun) - any organism that lives by eating or consuming other organisms

Proboscis (proh-bos-is or proh-bos-kis, noun) - the long, protruding mouthpart of insects, adapted specifically for sipping in butterflies

Pupa (pyoo-puh, noun) - a phase during which transformation takes place and the organism stops eating and remains still; the 3rd stage of the butterfly life cycle involving the chrysalis and metamorphosis

Species (spee-seez, noun) - a group of individuals having common features and the most basic of ways to categorize organisms

Structural scale (struhk-cher-uhl skeyl, noun) - a thin, plate that covers butterfly wings and creates intense and iridescent colors by refracting and diffracting light

Thorax (thohr-aks, noun) - in insects, the 2nd part of the body between the head and the abdomen and the body part to which the wings and legs attach

Warm-blooded (wawrm-bluhd-id, adjective) - animals whose body temperature stays the same no matter how hot or cold the temperature of their environment gets

Beautiful and graceful,
varied and enchanting,
small but approachable,
butterflies lead you
to the sunny side of life.

- Jeffrey Glassberg

www.ingramcontent.com/pod-product-compliance
Lightning Source LLC
Chambersburg PA
CBHW050826290526
45792CB00001B/278